SPEECH.

FELLOW-CITIZENS:

Called to preside over this annual Convention, where are brought together the intelligence, the heart and the conscience of Massachusetts, God bless her! I begin by asking you to accept my thanks. Gladly would I leave this post of honor to another; but I obey your will, In all I have to say I must speak frankly. What has with me become a habit is at this moment more than ever a duty. Who can see peril to his country, and not cry out? Who can see that good ship, which carries the Republic and its fortunes, driving directly upon a lee-shore, and not shout to the pilot, "Mind your helm?" Apologies or roundabout phrases are out of place when danger threatens.

EMANCIPATION NOT COMPLETE, SO LONG AS THE BLACK CODE EXISTS.

When last I addressed my fellow-citizens on public affairs, at the close of the late Presidential election, as we were about to vote for Abraham Lincoln and Andrew Johnson, I undertook to show the absolute identity between Slavery and the Rebellion, so that one could not end without the other. As I finished that address, I said to friends near me, that it was "my last Anti-Slavery speech." I so thought at the time; for I anticipated the speedy downfall of the Rebellion, carrying with it Slavery. I was mistaken. Neither the Rebellion or Slavery is yet ended. The Rebellion has been disarmed; but that is all. Slavery has been abolished in name; but that is all. As there is still a *quasi* Rebellion, so is there still a *quasi* Slavery. The work of liberation is not yet completed. Nor can it be completed until the Equal Rights of every person, once claimed as a slave, are placed under the safeguard of irreversible guarantees. It is not enough to strike down the master; you must also lift up the slave. It is not enough to declare Emancipation. The whole Black Code, which is the supplement of Slavery, must give place to that Equality before the law, which is the very essence of Liberty. It is an old principle of the common law, recognized by all our courts, as announced by Lord Coke, that "where the law granteth anything to any one, that also is granted, without which the thing itself cannot be." So also where a piece of land is granted, which is shut in by the possessions of the grantor, a *right of way* is implied from common justice and the necessity of the case. And then again, where the reason of a law ceases, the law itself ceases. So, also, where the principal falls to the ground, the incident falls also. But all these unquestionable principles are fatal to the Black Code. The Liberty that has been granted "cannot be" if the Black Code exists. The piece of land that has been granted, is useless without that right of way which is stopped up by the Black Code. The reason for the Black Code is Slavery; and with the cessation of the reason, the whole Black Code itself must cease also. The Black Code is the incident of Slavery, and it must fall with its principal. Unless this is accomplished, you will keep the word of promise to the ear and break it to the sense. You will imitate those cruel quibbles, of which history makes mention, where, by subtle equivocations, faith has been violated. You will do little better than the Turk, who stipulated with a certain person that his head should be safe, and straightway proceeded to cut him in two at the middle; or than those false Greeks who, after promising to restore their captives, kept their promise by restoring them dead.

Slavery begins by denying the right of a man to himself; and the Black Code fortifies this denial by its cruel exclusions. Every freedman must be secured in this right by his admission to the full panoply of citizenship. Slavery sets at naught the relation of husband and wife. Every freedman must be able to call his wife his own. Slavery sets at naught the parental relation. Every freedman must be able to call his child his own. Slavery shuts the gates of knowledge. Every freedman must be assured in all the privileges of education. Slavery takes from its victim the hard-earned fruits of his toil. Every freedman must be protected in his industry. Slavery denies justice to the colored man by cruelly rejecting his testimony. Every freedman must enter the courts freely, as witness or as party. Until all this is done, in every particular, and beyond possibility of question, it is vain to say that Emancipation has been secured. *The good work is only half done.* It must be continued to its assured consummation, under the powerful auspices of the United States. That same National authority which began it must take care that the good work is maintained and completed, in letter and in spirit, everywhere throughout the rebel States,—in conventions of the people,—in legislative assemblies,—in courts,—in the city,—in the country,—in streets,—on highways,—on by-ways,—in retired places,—on plantations,—in houses,—so that no man shall be despoiled of any of his rights, but all shall be Equal before the law.

Lesson from Russian Emancipation.

There is a glorious instance in our own day, which is an example for us, when the Emperor of Russia, by a Proclamation, fulfilling the aspirations of his predecessors, set free twenty-three millions of serfs, and then completed his work by *supplementary provisions* investing the freedmen with civil and political rights, including the right to testify in court; the right of suffrage; and the right to hold office. I have in my hand this immortal Proclamation, dated at St. Petersburg, 19th February, 1861; promulgated amidst prayers and thanksgivings in all the churches of the national capital, and at once expedited to every part of the widely-extended empire by generals and staff officers of the Emperor himself. Here it is, in an official document entitled *Affranchissement des Serfs*, and issued at St. Petersburg. After reciting that the earlier measures in behalf of the serfs had failed, because they had been left to "the spontaneous initiative of the proprietors," the Emperor proceeds to take the work in hand as a sacred legacy from his ancestors, and declares the serfs, after an interval of two years, "entirely enfranchised." Meanwhile, that nothing might fail, "a special court" for serfs was created in each province, charged with the organization of local governments, the adjustment of boundaries, and generally to superintend the transition from the Old to the New, with "justices of the peace" in each district, to examine on the spot all questions arising from Emancipation. Had the work stopped here, it would have been incomplete. *It would have been only half done.* But no such fatal mistake was made.*

Accompanying the Proclamation, are *supplementary provisions*, called "regulations," prepared with infinite care, and divided into chapters and sections—occupying no less than ninety-one pages in double columns and small type—by which the rights of the freedmen are secured beyond question. Beginning with the declaration that the freedmen "acquire the rights belonging to the condition of free farmers," they then proceed in formal words to fix and assure their rights, civil and political. By one section, it is provided that "the articles of the Civil Code on the rights and obligations of the family, are extended to the freedmen; that consequently they acquire the right, without the authorization of the proprietor, to contract marriage, and to make any arrangement whatever concerning their family affairs; that they can equally enter into all agreements and obligations authorized by the laws, as well with the State as with individuals, on the conditions established for free farmers; that they can inscribe themselves in the guilds, and exercise their trades in the villages; and they can found and conduct factories and establishments of commerce." Another section secures to the freedmen the right of acquiring and alienating property of all kinds, according to the general law, and besides, guarantees, on certain conditions, "the possession of their homesteads," with the grounds appurtenant. Another section secures to the freedmen complete *Equality in the courts*, with "the right of action, whether civilly or criminally, to commence process, and to answer personally or by attorney; to make complaint, and to defend their rights by all the means known to the law, *and to appear as witnesses and as bail, conformably to the common law.*" Other sections secure to the freedmen *Equality in political rights*, by providing that "on the organization of the towns, they shall be entitled to take part in the meetings and elections for the towns, and to vote on town affairs, and to exercise divers functions;" that they shall also "take part in the assemblies for the district, and shall vote on district affairs, and choose the chairman," and generally enjoy all rights to choose their local officers and to be chosen in turn. And still another section authorizes the freedmen "to place their children in the establishments for public education, to embrace the career of instruction, or the scientific career, or to take ser-

* At this stage of his speech Mr. Sumner called attention to M. Kapnist, a Russian gentleman belonging to the Chancery of the Emperor, who was on the platform. The allusion was received by the Convention with applause, which M. Kapnist acknowledged by rising and bowing.

vice in the corps of surveyors." And it is further provided, that they "cannot lose their rights or be restrained in their exercise, except after judgment of the town, according to fixed rules." And still further, that they "cannot be subjected to any punishment, otherwise than by virtue of a judgment, or according to the legal decision of the town to which they belong." Such are the safeguards by which Emancipation in Russia has been completed and assured. Such is the lesson of the great Empire to the great Republic.

Duty of Massachusetts.

In asking that we shall do likewise, I follow the plain suggestions of reason, whether we regard the interest of the freedman or our own. But justice to the freedman is now intimately linked with the national security. Be just, and the Republic will be strong. Be just, and you will erect a barrier against the Rebellion. On this question Massachusetts has a duty to perform. Now, as in times past, her place is in the front. You will not, I trust, be disturbed by criticism, even if it become invective. Throughout the long conflict with Slavery, and the earlier conflict with the mother country, Massachusetts has become accustomed to hard words, and, even at a more ancient day, as far back in colonial history as 1691, we find an ill-tempered critic, with a strange jumble of metaphors, crying out against our fathers, "All the frame of heaven moves upon one axis, and the whole of New England interest seems designed to be loaden on one bottom and her particular motion to be concentric to the Massachusetts tropic. You know who are wont to trot after the Bay horse." If others trot after the Bay horse, it is simply because Massachusetts means always to keep on the right road, and, by unerring instinct, knows the way. Error proceeds oftener from ignorance than from malice. Obviously, at this moment, the great difficulty is that people do not see clearly what ought to be done.

National Security.

Fellow-citizens, as peace seems about to smile on our country, convulsed by most cruel and costly war, there is one simple duty on which all can unite when it is understood. It is the duty expressed in at least one part of the familiar saying, "Indemnity for the past and *security for the future.*" Indemnity, alas! we can never have. Who can repay the millions of lost treasure? Who can repair the shattered and mutilated forms that have been returned from the battle with Slavery? Who can recall the dead? Indemnity we renounce. There are no scales on earth in which it can be weighed. There are no possible accumulations of wealth which would not be exhausted before its first instalment was counted out. But no such difficulty can occur in adjusting our security for the future. And the very vastness of our sacrifice is an irresistible reason why this should be fixed beyond question, so that the terrible judgment shall not visit us again. Indemnity we renounce; *but security we will have.* This is the one thing needful. This is the charity which embraces all other charities. This is the pivot of the national Hereafter. This is at once the corner-stone and the key-stone of that reconstructed Union, to which we look for tranquil peace and reconciliation. There are none so high, and there are none so low, as not to be concerned in obtaining this security, for without it all that we hold most dear will be in jeopardy. Without security agriculture and commerce must languish and die; without security the whole country must be impoverished in its resources, while the rich become poor and the poor become poorer; without security rights of property and rights of person will lose their value; and without security the Union, justice, domestic tranquillity, the common defence, the general welfare, and the blessings of Liberty, for which the Constitution was ordained and established, must all fail! What is government, or country, or home, or life itself, without security?

National Faith.

There is another object, kindred to security, or, perhaps, embraced in security; and that is the *national faith.* This too must be placed beyond cavil or even "suspicion." No nation can be powerful enough to disregard this sacred bond. Character, fame, and prosperity itself are all dependent upon its observance. But the national faith is solemnly engaged, first, to the national freedmen, and secondly, to the national creditors. No undertaking can be more complete and inviolable because it constituted the consideration for those services and supplies by which the life of the Republic has been preserved. The national faith is pledged to the national freedmen, not only by the act of Emancipation, which, in its very essence and from the nature of the case, is a "warranty of title," but also by the plain and positive promises of the Proclamation, that they "*are and henceforward shall be free*, and that the Executive government of the United States, including the military and naval authority thereof, will recognize and *maintain the freedom of such persons.*" Words could not be more binding, and the history of their introduction testifies to their significance and efficacy. They were not in the original draft by President Lincoln, but were inserted, at the suggestion of Mr. Seward, when the Proclamation was read to the Cabinet; and there they stand without any limitation of place or time, binding this Republic in its national character, through its Executive, including the military and naval authority, not only to recognize, but to *maintain* the freedom of the emancipated slave; and this is to be done, not in any special locality, but everywhere, and not for a day or a year, but for all time. Our obligation to the national creditors is of the same validity, approved by successive acts of Congress, ratified by the popular will, and fixed beyond recall by the actual enjoyment of those precious fruits for which the debt was incurred. Repudiation of our bonds, whether to the national creditors or to the national freedmen, would be a shame and a crime; and the national faith is irrevocably plighted to the two alike. Here is the Proclamation, and here is a Treasury Note. Look at the signatures and look at the terms. The former is signed by the President himself, Abraham Lincoln; the latter is signed by an unknown clerk, whose name I cannot decypher. The former is stronger, and more positive in its terms, than the latter. The Treasury Note simply says; "It is hereby certified that the United States are indebted unto ——— bearer in the sum of $100, redeemable" after a certain date, and that "this debt is authorized by Act of Congress." The binding terms of the Proclamation, which I have already read, are solemnly enforced by that memorable invocation at the close: "And upon this act, sincerely believed to be an act of justice warranted by the Constitution upon military necessity, I invoke the considerate judgment of mankind and the gracious favor of Almighty God." Thus religion comes to confirm the pledge with sanctions of its own. That pledge is as enduring as the Republic itself.

Such are the supreme objects now at heart—the *National Security and the National Faith*, or the two absorbed into one, *Security for the Future.*

The Dikes of Holland.

And here allow me to present an illustration, which, unless I mistake, will make our duty clear. You do not forget the immense and costly dikes, built by Holland against the sea; but, perhaps, you may not call to mind their origin and importance. Before these embankments were constructed the whole country was in constant danger. At an early period there was an irruption which destroyed no less than forty-four villages, followed very soon by another which destroyed eighty thousand lives. In the 15th century there was still another which swept away one hundred thousand persons—a terrible sacrifice, even greater in proportion to the population of Holland at that time, than what we have been called to bear from the bloody irruption of slavery. At last the dikes were constructed as safeguards, and down to this day they are preserved at a large annual cost. Precautions of all kinds are superadded. A special corps of engineers, educated at Delft, is constantly employed in the work of renovation. Watchmen patrol the walls, and alarm bells are ready to ring. The gratitude of the people shows itself even to its unconscious protectors; and the stork, which, resting here on his flight from Africa, destroys the vermin that weaken and sap the dikes, is held in veneration, so that to kill a stork is looked upon as little less than a crime. Such are some of the defences, by which Holland is guarded against danger from the sea. But how petty is her danger compared with ours! We too must have our dikes, with engineers to keep them strong—with watchmen to patrol them—with alarm bells to ring; and we too must have our storks to destroy the vermin that weaken and sap our embankments.

Our Dikes are Guarantees.

What shall be our defences? How shall we guard against destructive irruptions? And where shall we establish our security for the future? Our embankments must not be of earth. Walls of stone will not do. Towers, ramparts and buttresses will be impotent against our vindictive tide. The security we seek must be found in *organic law with irreversible guarantees; and these irreversible guarantees must be co-extensive with the danger.*

Elements of Danger.

It becomes us, then, to consider carefully the elements of danger,—bearing in mind always that a danger clearly foreseen will not happen, unless prudence has ceased to prevail. These elements may be considered in general and in detail. They may be considered in certain general influences, applicable to all our relations with the Rebellion, or in certain specific points, which obviously require specific guarantees.

If we look at the rebel States generally, there is little to inspire trust. They rose against a paternal government simply for the sake of Slavery, planting themselves upon two postulates furnished by John C. Calhoun—first, State rights; and secondly, the alleged falsehood of our fathers, when, at the birth of our nation, they declared that all men are born equal. Since that early war when Satan "in proud rebellious arms, drew after him the third part of Heaven," nothing so utterly wicked has occurred. And the spirit of Satan entered into the Rebellion, and continued with it to the end. It was present on the battle-field. It was present in the treatment of Union prisoners. It was present in the piracies of the ocean. I know not that these devils have yet been cast out. I know not that any swine into which they have entered have rushed headlong into the sea. But I do know that, according to concurring and unimpeachable testimony, from all quarters of the rebel States,—from North Carolina to Texas,—there is one sullen, defiant voice, which, in the very words of Satan when driven from the skies, thus speaks:—

> "What though the field be lost?
> All is not lost; the unconquerable will,
> And study of revenge, immortal hate,—
> And courage never to submit or yield.
> Since through experience of this great event,
> In arms not worse, in foresight much advanced,
> We may with more successful hope resolve
> To wage by force *or guile* eternal war,
> Irreconcilable to our grand foe."

Such is their spirit. Grounding their arms, they now resort to other means. Cunning takes the place of war. As they precipitated themselves out of the Union, they now seek to precipitate themselves back. A "wooden horse" is constructed, which is stuffed with hidden foes, and thus they seek to enter our Troy. Already the rattle of arms is heard, and ominous voices, as the treacherous engine is advanced. But beyond these sounds, there is the record of the past and the present. Who does not know that the South is full of spirits, who have sworn undying hatred not only to the Union, but to reason itself, and whose policy is a perpetual conspiracy against the principles of our government? Painful proofs come to demonstrate the prevailing frenzy. The freedmen are trodden down and the land is filled with tragedies. History stands aghast at the massacre of Glencoe in a retired Scotch valley, and our sympathies overflow at the murder of a solitary traveller by the merciless Indians; but these scenes are now repeated. The Barbarism of Slavery rages still. The lash and the bloodhound are at large. Life is little, if it beats under a colored skin. Citizens in the national uniform are insulted, mutilated, murdered—especially if they are in command of colored troops. And these criminals, besmeared with blood, and boiling with concentrated rage, now strive to envelop themselves in the immunities of State Independence, with two special objects in view: first, that they may deal with the freedmen as they please, without any check from the National authority; and, secondly, that they may send a solid representation of more than eighty votes, pledged to Southern pretensions, which, in combination with treacherous votes from the North, may re-assert that ancient monopoly and masterdom under which the country suffered so long;

> "and once more
> Erect the standard there of ancient night."

Reading the proceedings of the convention in Mississippi, we seem again to hear the very voice of Satan:

> "To claim our just inheritance of old,
> Whether by open war or *covert guile*,
> We now debate."

One of their speakers said plainly, that "he was opposed to fighting the General Government or anybody else; *that he was ready to submit to its wishes as he would to a highway robber, whose power he was not able to resist.*" Another speaker, less frank, thought it policy to accept the present condition of affairs, until the control of the State is restored into the hands of its people, and "to submit *for a time* to evils which cannot be remedied." And still another, much more wily, when urging a seeming acceptance of the Union, thus lured his brother conspirators: "*If we act wisely we shall be joined by what is called the Copperhead party,* and even by many of the Black Republicans." Such is the plot, and such is the disastrous alliance plainly foreshadowed. But, thank God! in encouraging his comrades the conspirator has warned us. Forewarned is forearmed.

The National Debt Threatened.

From all quarters comes the warning. "Trust not their presents, nor admit the horse!" The voice of the Grecian Sinon was not more treacherous. From all quarters comes the testimony. Military officers returning from the South, public functionaries, intelligent travellers, loyal residents, each and all speak with one voice. By conversation and by letter I have gathered the proofs which are complete. Persons who have had peculiar opportunities unite in the report that the rebel spirit still prevails, — that the treatment of the freedmen is beastly, — and that the national debt is denounced. Two eminent gentlemen, whose official positions have made them familiar with public opinion in two different States, have expressed to me the conviction that there was *not a single ex-rebel who would vote to pay the interest on the national debt.* A trustworthy traveller, who has just visited Louisiana, Mississippi, and Alabama, with which he was already familiar, writes me: "The former masters exhibit a most cruel, remorseless, and vindictive spirit towards the colored people. In parts where there are no Union soldiers, I saw colored women treated in the most outrageous manner. They have no rights that are respected. They are killed, and their bodies thrown into ponds or mud-holes. They are mutilated by having ears and noses cut off." A loyalist from Texas writes: "What we of the South fear is, that President Johnson's course will, by its *precipitancy,* enable the old set to re-organize themselves into place and power. For Heaven's sake preserve us, if you can, from this calamity." A loyal resident of North Carolina thus writes: "I tell you, sir, the only difference now and one year ago is that the flag is acknowledged as supreme, and there is some fear manifested, and they have no arms. The sentiment is the same. If anything otherwise, more hatred exists towards the government. *I know there is more towards Union men, both black and white.*" It is natural that such a people should already talk of repudiating the national debt. Here is a bit on this vital point. A young man in gray was asked, "Would it be safe to trust white men at the South with the power to repudiate the national debt?" To which he replied at once: "Repudiate! I should hope they would. I'm whipped, and I'll own it; but I'm not so fond of a whipping that I'm going to pay a man's expenses while he gives it to me. Of course, there are not ten men in the whole South that wouldn't repudiate!" Thus spoke the rebel uniform. But here are the grave words of a candidate for Congress in Virginia, in his address to the people:—

"I am opposed to the Southern States being taxed at all for the redemption of this debt, either directly or indirectly; and, if elected to Congress, I will oppose all such measures, and I *will vote to repeal all laws that have heretofore been passed for that purpose;* and, in doing so, I do not consider that I violate any obligation to which the South was a party. *We have never plighted our faith for the redemption of the war debt.* The people will be borne down with taxes for years to come, even if the war debt is repudiated. It will be the duty of the government to support the maimed and disabled soldiers, and this will be a great expense; and, if the United States Government requires the South to be taxed for the support of Union soldiers, we should insist that all disabled soldiers should be maintained by the United States Government, *without regard to the side they had taken in the war.*"

Irreversible Guarantees.

Again, I say, forewarned is forearmed. Surely there can be no limits to our resistance when such spirits are seeking to capture the National Government; but beyond that general resistance, which must make us postpone the day of surrender, and invoke the protection of Congress, we must insist upon *special guarantees* in the organic law.

I.—The Unity of the Republic.

(1.) As the Rebellion began with the pretension that a State might withdraw from the Union, it is plain that the *Unity of the Republic* must be affirmed—not indirectly but directly; not as in Mississippi, by simply declaring the late act of secession null and void; but, as in Missouri, where the relations of the State to the Union are thus frankly stated: "That this State shall ever remain a member of the American Union; *that the people thereof are a part of the American Nation;* that every citizen owes paramount allegiance to the Constitution and Government of the United States; and that no law or ordinance of this State, in contravention or subversion thereof, can have any binding force." In contrast with this plain renunciation, the proceedings of Mississippi have no more certainty than the common saying, "Large as a piece of chalk." As security for the future, they are nothing—absolutely nothing. And permit me to say, that the whole Convention, so far as we have been informed, was little better than a rebel conspiracy to obtain political power.

II.—Enfranchisement.

(2.) As the Rebellion was waged in denial of the *Equal Rights* of the colored race, it is essential not only that Slavery should be renounced, but also that all men should be hailed as equal before the law, and this enfranchisement must be both civil and political. Unless this is done, the condition of the freedman will be most deplorable. Exposed to all manner of brutality, he will not be heard as a witness against his oppressor. Compelled to pay taxes, he will be excluded from all representation in the government. Without this security, Emancipation is illusory. It is a jack-a-lantern, which the poor slave will pursue in vain. Even if Slavery cease to exist, it will give place to another condition hardly less galling. There will be serfdom, apprenticeship, peonage or some other device of Slavery. According to the poet, there are different "circles" in hell, each with its own terrible torments, and the unhappy African will only escape from one of these into another. And all this will be beyond correction or remedy, if not at the outset guarded against by organic law.

III.—The National Debt.

(3.) As the *national debt* was incurred for the suppression of the Rebellion, this too must be fixed beyond repeal. Unless this is done, it is evident, from reason as well as from testimony, that the representatives of the rebel States will coalesce with others for its repudiation. Mississippi, which leads in the present effort to capture the national capital, is the original author of repudiation. Out of the legislative halls of this State the monster sprang. There was its birth. It will be simply true to its past history, as well as to its present animosities, when this State leads in the repudiation of the national debt. Nothing short of madness will allow it any such opportunity. No rebel State should be re-admitted unless bound irrevocably to the support of the national debt and the payment of the interest thereon.

IV.—Assumption of the Rebel Debt must be Forbidden.

(4.) The *assumption of the rebel debt* must be positively forbidden. Already ex-rebels insist upon its payment. Such voices come from Mississippi and Virginia. Ex-rebel newspapers, whose editors have taken the oath of allegiance, uphold this debt. But Congress has already led the way in denouncing it. For a State to assume this criminal obligation would be oppressive to the people, and especially to the freedmen. It would be a drain upon the resources of the State. It would be an insult to the whole country. This debt, whether at home or abroad, has been incurred for the support of the Rebellion and must be treated accordingly. It is a part of the crime. Here too there must be a guarantee.

V.—National Peace and Tranquillity, through Impartial Suffrage.

(5.) As the *national peace and tranquillity* depend essentially upon the overthrow of monopoly and tyranny, here is another occasion for a special guarantee against the whole pretension of color. No rebel State can be re-admitted with this controversy still raging, and ready to break forth. So long as it continues the land will refuse its increase. Agriculture and business of all kinds will be uncertain, and the country will be handed over to a fearful struggle with the terrors of St. Domingo to darken the prospect. In shutting out the freedman from his equal rights at the ballot-box, you open the doors of discontent and insurrection. Cavaignac, the patriotic President of the French Republic, met the present case, when, speaking for France, he said: "I do not believe repose possible, either in the present or the future, except so far as you found your political condition on universal suffrage, loyally, sincerely, completely accepted and observed." (*Moniteur*, 21 May, 1850, p. 1761.) It is only *impartial suffrage* that I claim, without distinction of color, so that there shall be one equal rule for all men. And this too must be placed under the safeguard of constitutional law.

VI.—Education of the People.

(6.) As the *Education of the people* is essential to the national welfare, and especially to the development of those principles of justice and morality which constitute the only sure foundation of a "republican government," and as, according to the census, an immense proportion of the people of the rebel States, without distinction of color, cannot read and write, it is obvious that public schools must be established for the equal good of all. The example of Massachusetts must be followed, which, after declaring in its Constitution that "wisdom and knowledge, as well as virtue, diffused generally among the body of the people, are necessary for the preservation of their rights and liberties," proceeds to direct the legislature and magistrates, in all future periods, "to cherish the interests of literature and the sciences," and especially "public schools and grammar schools in the towns." All this must enter into our work of reconstruction, and become one of our guarantees.

Necessity of these Guarantees.

Such are the six capital subjects of special guarantee: the unity of the Republic; the national obligations to the national freedmen; the national obligations to the national creditors; the rejection of the rebel debt; the establishment of national peace and tranquillity, so that it cannot be disturbed by any monopoly and tyranny founded on color; and lastly, the education of the people. All these are too important, too transcendent, to be left to the transient will of recent rebels, always ready to be excited; nor can they be left to any vague promise or inference of any kind. They must be fixed in characters clear as the sky, and firm as the earth itself. Not to require this protection is unpardonable weakness. "If Philip dies," said the Athenian orator, "you will soon raise another Philip; since it is not so much by his own power, as by your carelessness, that he grew to such greatness;" and so do I say now, even if the Rebellion is dead, you will soon raise another, unless you learn to be wise. Believe me, that man is dangerous who does not see danger in this rebel Oligarchy, now conspiring to hoist itself into power.

Power to establish Guarantees.

Therefore, I lay down one undeniable, essential principle—that these guarantees must be established; and I appeal to my fellow-citizens throughout the country to insist upon them. As they concern the National Security and the National Faith, it is clear that they should be established by the Nation. The object is national. The power to establish them is national also. It is a part of that great, instinctive right of *self-defence*, common to nations and to men, which has no limits, except in the benign constraints of a Christian civilization. It is a right not only from the Constitution of the United States, but also from the constitution of civil society itself. There is no nation without it. In the weakest it is as manifest as in the mightiest. Never before was the occasion for its exercise plainer. And who shall say that the Nation may defend itself on the murderous battle-field, and may not, when the battle has been won, require that "Security for the Future," which is the declared object of war?

Do you ask where in the Constitution this unquestionable power is to be found? I answer, in the same clause where you find the power to raise armies, and hurl them upon the rebel enemy; in the same clause where you find the power to erect fortifications, bastions, and bulwarks for the national defence; in the same clause where you find the power to incur the national debt for the national defence; and also in the same clause where President Lincoln found the power to emancipate the slave. It is a National power for the protection of the Nation, and it may be exercised to any extent needed. It is idle to say that the war is over, and, therefore, the power is suspended. In one sense the war is over, and in another it is not. Battles have ceased; but "Security for the Future" has not yet been obtained, and this security is found only in irreversible guarantees.

This national power is at this moment in full operation, and as completely constitutional as the power to raise armies. It assumes for the present purpose two forms: first, the power to hold military possession of the rebel States, so long as is required for security, whether months or years; and, secondly, the power to affix the terms of peace and restoration. As it is idle to say that the war is over, so it is equally idle to say that this power, in either of its forms, is limited by the Constitution. This same mistake was made by James Buchanan, when, at the beginning of the Rebellion, he weakly declared, that, under the Constitution, he could not "coerce a State," and his Cabinet assented to the fatal pretension. God forbid that now, at another moment not less critical, this same pretension should triumph again. Of course all patriots now see how the golden opportunity was lost at first. May no such golden opportunity be lost again! Nobody now doubts that a State in rebellion may be "coerced." Nobody now doubts that the victories of Grant, the march of Sherman, aud the charge of Sheridan were strictly constitutional. But this "coercion" must endure just so long as may be needed to obtain "Security for the Future,"—it may be for months or it may be for years. There is no argument for it at the beginning which is not equally strong for it now. There is nothing in the Constitution against it. Everything in the Constitution is for it. The rules or limitations which the Constitution may establish for a condition of peace are entirely in applicable to a condition of Rebellion in any of its stages, whether at its beginning, its middle or its end. Whatever is needed for the suppression of the Rebellion and the establishment of safeguards against its recurrence is constitutional. *It is the failure to exercise this power which is unconstitutional.*

But beyond this ample power, there are two other powers in the Constitution, by virtue of which all needful guarantees can be secured. The first is that vast untried power under the clause of the Constitution, declaring that "the United States shall guarantee to every State a republican form of government." This power, long dormant, sprang at once into activity with the acts of secession. Loyal government being overthrown *in fact*, so that the whole region was like an "empty slate," it became the duty of the National authority to set up loyal governments, and at the same time to see that they were "republican in form," which must mean at least that they are governments of the majority, and not of the minority; and I think I cannot err, if I add, that, according to the fundamental principles of the Declaration of Independence, they must be founded on the Equal Rights of all men and the "consent of the governed." It is very clear that in this clause of guarantee there is an inexhaustible power, by virtue of which the National authority can not only exact all needful guarantees, but can mould these rebel communities according to the model of a Christian Commonwealth.

There is still another source of power under the Constitution; and this is according to the analogies of the territories. Since all loyal government has ceased to exist, the whole region, in all its divisions and sub-divisions, has, from the *necessity of the case*, lapsed under the National jurisdiction, which is as complete for all practical purposes as that same jurisdiction over the District of Columbia.

But I do not stop to dwell on these sources of power. Elsewhere I have vindicated them, and I have never been answered, except by the phrase that a State cannot go out of the Union, as if, in presence of the *fact of rebellion*, this was anything more than a phrase. It is indisputable that, *in point of fact*, the rebel States have ceased to be, as President Lincoln expressed it, "in practical relations with the Union," and still further that they have long been without any government, which we can recognize. Surely this is enough to open the door to the National authority. When loyal government ceased, the jurisdiction of the National government began, whether military or civil, and this jurisdiction still continues, complete in all respects, without any hindrance or limitation from the Constitution.

Thus, out of three inexhaustible fountains may the National government derive its authority; first, from the War Powers, which do not expire except with the establishment of "Security for the Future;" secondly, from the injunction to guarantee a Republican form of government, which is at once a power and a duty; and, thirdly, from the necessity of the case, as with outlying territories, which have no other government. Under each and all of these powers the guarantees can be obtained.

Practical Points.—Ways not to obtain Guarantees.

In obtaining these guarantees there are certain practical points which must not be disregarded. Knowing what we need and satisfied with regard to the powers of the National government, the path will be easy. As there are ways to obtain guarantees, so, also, there are ways not to obtain them.

And, first, of the ways not to obtain them.

(1.) Irreversible guarantees cannot be obtained by *haste*. No State must be precipitated back to the Union. Precipitation back will be hardly less fatal than that original precipitation which plunged the country into the abyss of war. When a State is re-admitted, it becomes practically independent. Therefore prudence, care and watchfulness will be needed to see that the National interests are not imperilled by any sudden transformation.

(2.) Irreversible guarantees cannot be obtained merely by Executive action. Something more is needed. No President can safely say, "The State—it is I." He is only a part of the State, and, on this account, there is a new motive to reserve. What he does is subject to the correction of Congress, and therefore cannot be final.

(3.) Irreversible guarantees cannot be obtained *by yielding to the prejudice of color*, and *insisting upon a separation of the races.* A voice from the West—God save the West!—revives the exploded theory of colonization, partly to divert attention from the great question of Equal Rights. To that voice I reply, first, you ought not to do it, and, secondly, you cannot do it. You ought not to do it, because, besides its intrinsic and fatal injustice, you will thus deprive the country of what it most needs, which is labor. Those freedmen on the spot are better even than mineral wealth. Each is a mine, out of whom riches can be drawn, provided you let him share the product. And through him that general industry will be established which is better than any thing but virtue, and is, indeed, a form of virtue. It is vain to say that this is the country of the "white man." It is the country of Man. Whoever disowns any member of the Human Family as Brother, disowns God as Father, and thus becomes impious as well as inhuman. It is the glory of Republican Institutions that they give practical form to this irresistible principle. If any body is to be sent away, let it be the guilty, and not the innocent. The expatriation of leading rebels will be a public good. As long as they continue here, they will resist the establishment of guarantees; but it is little short of madness to think of exiling loyal persons, whose strong arms are needed, not only for the cultivation of the soil, but also for the protection of the government itself.

(4.) Irreversible guarantees cannot be obtained by *oaths.* All oaths are uncertain. It has been said "the strongest oaths are straw." Political oaths have become a proverb, whether in England or France. They have been taken freely, and have been broken without hesitation. The Milanese, in reply to the Emperor Barbarossa, said, "You had our oath, but we never swore to keep it." Our rebels have been openly taught the same duplicity. They have been told authoritatively, that the oath was unconstitutional, and, therefore, not binding; and so they take it easily. But who can find a guarantee in such a performance? A Swedish priest lately poisoned the sacramental wine, and so these counsellors have poisoned this sacred obligation. But if an oath be taken, it must not stop with the support of the Proclamation of Emancipation. It must embrace all those other objects of guarantee, including especially the National freedmen and the National creditors. Each of these will be a *test of loyalty.* But at a moment like the present, at the close of a ferocious rebellion, when hatred and passion are only pent up and not extinguished, an oath is little better than a cotton thread to hold a frigate scourged by a north-wester. The Hollanders might as well undertake to swear each individual wave that beats upon their coasts. They did better. They made dikes. "Gone to swear a peace," says Constance, most scornfully, as she denounced an oath of pretended reconciliation. And shall we be content merely when our rebels "swear a peace?"

(5.) Irreversible guarantees cannot be obtained by *pardons*. It is enough to state this proposition; for all must see at once that rights will be very uncertain if they have no protection except in the gratitude of a pardoned rebel. A jail-delivery is not a guarantee. Such a breakwater would be impotent against the malignant sea. Without accepting absolutely the dogma of Cardinal Mazarin, that men are governed more through hope than through gratitude, it is clear that, until security is won, we cannot afford to part with any influence or agency through which control may be established. Mercy is a beautiful prerogative, exercised always with inexpressible delight; but on this account we must guard against its fascination, and not, in the generous luxury, imperil a whole community. This is very clear. A pardon is in form an act of grace, but in reality a letter of license. This is all. It leaves the criminal free to renew his crime, whether by force or guile. It has in it no single point of security. As well defend a citadel by kisses or by flowers.

Ways to Obtain Guarantees.

Such are some of the modes to be rejected. And now, in the second place, consider the ways in which guarantees may be obtained.

(1.) *Time is necessary.* There must be no precipitation. Time is the gentlest, but most powerful, revolutionist. Time is the surest reformer. Time is a peace-maker. Time is necessary to growth, and it is an element of change. For thirty years and more this wickedness was maturing. Who can say that the same time will not be needed now to mature the conditions of permanent peace? Who can say that a generation must not elapse before these rebel communities have been so far changed as to become safe associates in a common government? Plainly, this cannot be done at once. Wellington exclaimed at Waterloo, "Would that night or Blucher had come!" Time alone was a substitute for a powerful ally. It was more through time than battle that La Vendée was changed into loyalty. Time, therefore, we must have. Through time all other guarantees may be obtained; but time itself is a guarantee.

(2.) *Meanwhile we must follow Congress in the present exclusion of all rebels from political power.* They must not be voted for, and they must not vote. On this principle I take my stand. Let them buy and sell; let them till the ground; and may they be industrious and successful. These things they may do; but they must not be admitted at once into the co-partnership of our government. As well might the respectable Mr. Ketchum re-instate his son at once in the firm which he has betrayed, and invest him again with all the powers of a co-partner. The father received his son with parental affection, and forgave him; but he did not invite the criminal to resume his former desk in Wall Street. And yet Edward Ketchum, who had robbed and forged on an unprecedented scale, is as worthy of trust in the old banking-house as our rebels in the government of the country. A long probation will be needed before either can be admitted to his former fellowship. The *state of outlawry* is the present condition of each, and this condition must not be hastily relaxed.

Congress has already set the example by excluding from "any office of honor or profit under the government of the United States," and also by excluding as counsellor at law, from any court of the United States, every person who has given "aid or countenance" to the Rebellion, or who has "sought or accepted any office whatever" under it, or who has yielded to it any "voluntary support." By this act, (July 2d, 1862,) and the supplementary act, all rebels are debarred from holding office under the United States or from practising in the courts of the United States. This exclusion, thus sanctioned by Congress, must be the pole-star of our National policy. *If rebels cannot be officers under our government, they ought not to be voters.* They should be politically disfranchised, purely and simply as a measure of necessary precaution, and in order to prepare the way for those guarantees which we seek. "Vipers cannot use their venom in the cold." These are words of political wisdom as well as of scientific truth, and a great Italian writer did not hesitate to inculcate from them the same lesson that I do now.

Surely recent rebels, who led in secession and held office under the Rebellion are poor engineers to rally these communities to the support of the National freedmen and the National creditors, and generally to the establishment of those guarantees which are essential to security. Reason and experience warn us to postpone our trust in any such persons. Overcome in battle, they wrap themselves in a mantle of loyalty, tied by an oath,

> "As they who, to be sure of Paradise,
> Dying, put on the weeds of Dominic,
> Or in Franciscan think to pass disguised."

But character is not changed in a day, and that "Southern heart," which was "fired" against the Union, still preserves its vindictive violence. Even if for a moment controlled, who can tell how long it will continue in this mood? There is an exquisite fable of La Fontaine, where a cat was transformed into a beautiful woman; but on the night of her marriage, hearing the sound of a mouse on the floor, she sprang from the bed with all her original feline nature; and so a rebel, transformed by political necromancy into a loyalist, will suddenly start in full cry to run down a National freedman or a National creditor. So strong is nature. Horace tells us: Drive it out with a pitch-fork and it will return. Therefore, I insist, do not put political trust in that man who has been engaged in warring upon his country. I do not ask his punishment. I would not be harsh. There is nothing humane which I would reject. Nothing in hate. Nothing in vengeance. Nothing in passion. I am for gentleness. I am for a velvet glove; but I wish the hand for awhile of iron. I confess that I have little sympathy with those hypocrites of magnanimity, whose appeal for the rebel master is only a barbarous indifference towards the slave; and yet they cannot desire more than I do the day of reconciliation. To this end I am with them, *so far as is consistent with security;* but I cannot see my country sacrificed to a false idea. Pardon if you will. Nobody shall outdo me in clemency. But do not trust the rebel politically. The words of Shakspeare do not picture too strongly the danger of any such attempt:—

> "——— thou might'st hold a serpent by the tongue,
> A skinless lion by the mortal paw,
> A fasting tiger by the tooth,
> As keep in peace that hand which thou dost hold."

(4.) In obtaining guarantees we must rely upon acts rather than professions, and light our footsteps by "the lamp of experience." Therefore we turn from recent rebels to *constant loyalists*. This is only ordinary prudence. As those who have fought against us should be disfranchised, so those who have fought for us should be enfranchised, and thus a renovated state will be built secure on an unfaltering and natural loyalty. For awhile the freedman will take the place of the master, thus verifying the saying that the last shall be first and the first shall be last. In the pious books of the East it is declared, that the greatest mortification at the day of judgment will be when the faithful slave is carried to Paradise, and the wicked master is sent to hell; and this same reversal of conditions appears in the gospel when Dives is exhibited as suffering the pains of damnation while the beggar of other days is sheltered in Abraham's bosom. Therefore, in organizing this change we follow divine justice. Surely nobody can doubt that Robert Small, the heroic slave, who carried a rebel steamer to our fleet and then became our pilot, deserves more of the Republic than a South Carolina official, occupied at that very time as Commissioner to regulate impressments in the rebel army. To accept the latter and to reject the former will be not only the height of injustice, but the height of meanness. It will be a deed "to make heaven weep, all earth amazed."

(5.) Still further, in obtaining guarantees we must *look confidently to Congress*, which has plenary powers over the whole subject. Congress can do everything needful. It has already begun by excluding rebels from office. It must continue its jurisdiction; whether, through the War Powers, or the duty to guarantee a republican form of government, or the necessity of the case as in territories, is a matter of little importance. It is of less importance under which of its powers this is done, than that it is done. Continuing its jurisdiction, Congress must supervise and fix the conditions of order, so that the National Security and National Faith shall not suffer. Here is a sacred obligation which cannot be postponed.

(6.) All these guarantees should be completed and crowned by *an amendment of the Constitution of the United States*, especially providing that hereafter there shall be no denial of the electoral franchise or any exclusion of any kind, on account of color or race, but all persons shall be equal before the law. At this moment, under a just interpretation of the Constitution, three-fourths of the States actually coöperating in the National government, are sufficient for this change. The words of the Constitution are that amendments shall be valid to all intents and purposes, "when ratified by three-fourths of the legislatures of the several States," or, according to practical sense, *by three-fourths of the States that have legislatures*. If a State has no legislature, it cannot be counted in determining this quorum, as it is not counted in determining the quorum of either House of Congress, where precisely the same question occurs. Any other interpretation recognizes the Rebellion and plays into its hands by conceding its power, through rebellious contrivance, to prevent an amendment of the Constitution, essential to the general welfare.

Appeal to the President and Cabinet.

Such are practical points to be observed in obtaining the much-needed guarantees. Congress will soon be in session, and to its courageous conduct, in the exercise of unquestionable powers, we all look with hope and trust. Meanwhile the President, as commander-in-chief, has large military powers, which may be exercised without control until the meeting of Congress. To him I now appeal. Speaking from this platform —surrounded by this concourse of his friends—and giving voice to the sentiments of my heart, in harmony with the sentiments of Massachusetts, I cannot fail in respect or honor, while I address him with that plainness which belongs to Republican Institutions.

"Sir, your power is vast. A word from you may make an epoch. It may advance at once the cause of Universal Civilization, or it may quicken anew the Satanic energies of a fearful Barbarism. It may give assurance of security and reconciliation for the future, or it may scatter uncertainty and distrust, while it postpones that *Truce of God*, which is the longing of our hearts. As your power is vast, so is your responsibility. Act, we entreat you, so that our country may have no fresh sorrow. Do not hazard Emancipation, which is the day-star of our age, and the special jewel in the crown of your martyred predecessor, by any concession to its enemies. Do not put in jeopardy all that we hold most dear, by an untimely attempt to bring back into the copartnership of the National government, any of those ancient associates, who have warred upon their country. Let them wait. You have said that treason is "a crime," and not merely a difference of opinion. Do not let the criminals bear sway. The patriot dead cry out against such surrender, and all their wounds bleed afresh. Congress has already set the example, by declaring that no person engaged in the Rebellion shall hold office. For the present follow Congress. Follow the Constitution also, which knows no distinction of color, and do not sacrfice a whole race by resuscitating an offensive Black Code, inconsistent with the National Security and the National Faith. There also is the Declaration of Independence, which now shines like the sun in the Heavens, rejoicing to penetrate every bye-way and every cabin, if you will not stand in its light. Let it shine—until the Republic has completely conquered that disgusting pretension, which is at once a stupendous monopoly and an impious Caste. Above all, do not take from the loyal black man and give to the disloyal white man ; do not confiscate the political rights of the freedman, who has shed his blood for us, and lavish them upon his rebel master. And remember that justice to the colored race is the sheet-anchor of the national credit."

Speaking always with the same frankness, I ask leave to say briefly to the Secretary of War:—

"Sir, there is room still for your energies. That region, which has been won to Union and Liberty by the victory which you organized, must not be allowed to lapse under its ancient masters, the perjured asserters of property in man. It must not be abandoned. Let it be held by arms, until it smiles with the charities of life and all its people are guarded by an impenetrable shield."

And still speaking with the same frankness, I ask leave to press one controlling consideration upon the Secretary of the Treasury:—

"Sir, you are the guardian of the national finances. Use the peculiar influence which belongs to this position, so that nothing shall be done to impair the national credit. See to it especially that no person in any rebel community is admitted to political power who spurns the National Faith, sacredly plighted to the national freedman as well as to the national creditor. Such is the ordinance of Providence, that the fortunes of the two are joined inseparably together. Credit is sensitive. It needs that all the resources of the country should be brought into activity—that agriculture should be fostered—that commerce should be revived—that emigration should be encouraged; but this cannot be done without that *security* which is found in equal laws and a contented people. The farmer, the merchant, the emigrant, must each feel secure. Land, capital and labor are of little value, except on this essential condition. The loyal people, who have contributed so much, and now hold your bonds, trust that this essential condition will not fail through any failure on your part, and that you will not consent to open a political volcano, spouting with smoke and red-hot lava, in an extended region whose first necessity is peace. There is an order in all things, and any concession to the criminal enemies of our country, until after the confirmation of the National Security and the National Faith, is simply an illustration on a gigantic scale of the cart before the horse."

For myself, fellow-citizens, pardon me if I say that my course is fixed. Others may hesitate; others may turn away from those great truths, which make the far-reaching brightness of the Republic; others may seek a temporary favor by a temporary surrender. I shall not. The victory of blood, which has been so painfully won, must be confirmed by a greater victory of ideas, so that the renowned words of Abraham Lincoln may be fulfilled, and "this Nation under God shall have a new birth of Freedom, and government of the people, *by the people*, and for the people, shall not perish from the earth." To this end I seek no merely formal Union, seething with smothered curses, but a practical, moral, and political Unity, founded on common rights, knit together by common interests, inspired by a common faith, and throbbing with a common love of country,—where our Constitution, interpreted anew, shall be a covenant with life and a league with Heaven,—and Liberty shall be everywhere not only a right but a duty. John Brown, on his way to the scaffold, stooped to take up a slave child. That closing example was the legacy of the dying man to his country. That benediction we must continue and fulfil. The last shall be first; and so, in this new order, Equality, long postponed, shall become the master principle of our system and the very frontispiece of our Constitution. The Rebellion was to beat down this principle, by founding a government on the alleged "inferiority of a race." The attempt has failed, but not, alas! the insolent assumption of the conspirators. Taking up the gauntlet I now insist, that this assumption shall be trampled out. A righteous government cannot be founded on any exclusion of race. This is not the first time that I have battled with the Barbarism of Slavery. I battle still, as the bloody monster retreats to its last citadel, and, God willing, I mean "to fight it out on this line, if it takes" what remains to me of life.

www.ingramcontent.com/pod-product-compliance
Lightning Source LLC
LaVergne TN
LVHW020638110826
845149LV00004B/1260
9781418191047